Sara Rosenthal 88

The Nature in Close-up Series

1 The Life of a Butterfly
2 Newts
3 Food Chains
4 The Garden Spider
5 The Dragonfly
6 Honeybees
7 Insects we Need
8 Tree in a Wood
9 Moths
10 Owls
11 Life under Stones
12 Waterside Birds
13 Frogs and Toads
14 Wasps
15 Pond Life
16 Sea Birds
17 Foxes
18 Town Birds
19 Beetles
20 Snakes

Appleby, Leonard
Snakes.—(Nature in close-up; no.20)
1. Snakes—Juvenile literature
I. Title II. Series
597.96 QL666.06

ISBN 0-7136-2350-0

Published by A&C Black (Publishers) Limited
35 Bedford Row, London WC1R 4JH

First published 1983

ISBN 0-7136-2350-0

Filmset by August Filmsetting, Warrington, Cheshire
Printed in Hong Kong by Dai Nippon Printing Co. Ltd

Nature in Close-up

SNAKES

Leonard Appleby

Adam & Charles Black · London

Contents

Introduction

Do you think of snakes as slimy poisonous animals? If you've ever touched a snake, you'll know that they have dry skins. Many snakes are gentle and harmless, too. This book will tell you about many different kinds of snakes and how they live. But remember, never go near a snake unless you are with an adult and you are sure the snake is harmless.

Snakes belong to a group of animals called reptiles. Crocodiles, tortoises and lizards also belong to this group. You might have seen them in the reptile house at the zoo.

Rough-scaled sand boa, from ▶ India

Reptiles are *cold blooded* animals. This means that their bodies are heated by the temperature outside. They don't stay the same temperature all the time like we do.

Cold blooded animals will die if they get too hot or cold. This is why snakes don't live in very cold countries. There are more snakes in warm countries than in cool ones, like Britain. Snakes in cool countries have to sunbathe to keep warm.

▼British grass snake sunbathing

How snakes move

Snakes don't have arms or legs. They move their stomach muscles to push them along. When they want to move fast, snakes bend their bodies from side to side and zig-zag along the ground. Stones and rough ground don't hurt them because the snake's skin is covered in tough scales. Special large scales under their bodies help the snakes to move without slipping.

Adder looking for prey ▶

◀Boa constrictors spend much of their lives in trees

But snakes don't spend all their time on the ground. Many of them can climb trees. Snakes with long thin bodies are the best climbers. Some, like the mamba, spend most of their life in trees.

Many snakes can swim, too! They go into the water to find frogs or fish to eat. Others spend their whole lives in ponds, rivers or the sea. They swim by wriggling their bodies in the same way that snakes move along the ground. Sea snakes have a flattened tail, shaped like a paddle. This helps them to swim faster than any of the other water snakes.

◀The yellow anaconda from South America lives mainly in water. It feeds on water birds, small mammals and fish

▲ Skin of a puff adder

Skin shedding

Have you ever seen something like this lying in the grass? It is the old skin of a snake.

The snake's scaley outer skin is thin but very tough. It protects the softer skin underneath. But it doesn't grow as the snake gets bigger. Imagine having skin that gets too small for you! When this happens to a snake, its skin peels off and leaves a new skin underneath. We say the snake has shed its skin.

Adult snakes shed their skin from two to four times a year. Young snakes shed their skin more often because they're growing faster.

◀Yellow anaconda about to shed its skin

It's easy to tell when a snake is getting ready to shed its skin. The snake's colours go dull and its eyes turn a blueish-white colour. A few days later, the snake's eyes go clear again. Then the skin starts to peel back from the snake's head. The skin is pushed back along the body as the snake moves along. It comes off in one whole piece.

The snake looks very smart in its brand new skin. Its colours look bright and fresh as if they had just been painted on.

◀Yellow anaconda shedding its skin

Food and feeding

Snakes are meat eaters. But they don't have the right kind of teeth to chew their food like we do. Snakes have to swallow whole animals.

The biggest snakes can swallow a small deer or a young pig. A meal like this makes a huge bulge in the snake's body.

A snake can swallow an animal which is much bigger than its own head and wider than its body. This is because snakes can open their jaws very wide. A snake's skin is like elastic and stretches round large meals. After eating, a snake will yawn a few times to put its jawbones back into the right positions.

Snakes don't eat every day. If a snake has a very large meal, it might not be hungry again for a month. By keeping still and not using much energy, snakes can go without food for a long time. Pythons can live for more than two and a half years without food.

Brazilian rainbow boa swallowing a rat ▶

▲African puff adder yawning

▲African puff adder, about to swallow a rat

Seeing, hearing and smelling

Animals which eat meat need to have keen senses so they can find their prey. Snakes use their eyes, noses, tongues and bodies to find food.

Many snakes are short sighted. They can only see something clearly if it is nearby. But most of them are good at spotting sudden movement. This is very useful for catching animals. If an animal moves very slowly, a snake might not see it.

Vipers have two *poison fangs* at the front of the mouth. These fangs are like long, hollow teeth. When the snake bites, poison flows through each fang and out of a tiny hole near the point. When they aren't being used, a viper's poison fangs fold back along the roof of its mouth.

Cobras, mambas and coral snakes have slim bodies and small narrow heads. Their poison fangs are at the front of the mouth. These fangs are short and don't fold back.

Some snakes have their poison fangs at the back of the mouth. These fangs aren't hollow. The poison runs down a groove at the back of each fang. A few snakes of this kind have more than two poison fangs.

▲Adders yawn to fold their fangs back into the right place after they have killed their prey

▼The black mamba, from Africa, has a very powerful poison

Constrictors

Constricting snakes don't poison their prey. They squeeze it to death! The snake grabs an animal in its jaws and coils its body round the animal. This happens so quickly that it's hard to see just how it is done.

The snake tightens its coils around the animal's chest. It squeezes so tightly that the animal dies because it can't breathe. After smelling the animal with its tongue, the snake swallows its victim whole.

▼The blood python from New Guinea, constricting its prey. It can kill an animal within two or three minutes

▲Californian king snake swallowing a mouse it has constricted

All pythons and boas are constrictors. They are fatter than most snakes. Some of them are huge. The reticulated python of Asia can grow to more than ten metres long.

As well as pythons and boas, there are many other kinds of constrictors. The rat snakes and king snakes of North America are constrictors with slender bodies. They aren't usually more than two metres long.

The only constrictor in Britain is the smooth snake. It's only about half a metre long and lives on sandy heaths. There aren't many smooth snakes in Britain and you'd be lucky to see one.

Harmless snakes

Only a few kinds of snakes can kill animals by poison or constriction. Most of them have to swallow their prey while it is still alive. These snakes usually eat frogs, toads, newts and fish. Rodents or birds might peck or bite while they were being swallowed!

▼Grass snake swallowing a toad

Snakes which swallow their prey alive are often called harmless snakes. Most of them are gentle and would not hurt you. Some could give you a nasty bite if you got too close but they only do this because they are frightened. Not many of these snakes are over one and a half metres long.

The British grass snake swallows its prey alive. You might see one near a pond, looking for frogs and fish to eat. Grass snakes also live in damp woods and on commons.

The garter snake of North America ▶ is a harmless snake which feeds on amphibians and fish

Enemies and defence

Even poisonous snakes have enemies. They are eaten by some animals and by birds of prey, like eagles and hawks. Sometimes, snakes prey on each other. The king snake of North America is a constrictor that can kill rattlesnakes.

Snakes defend themselves in all sorts of different ways. Can you spot the adder in this picture? Its colours and markings blend in with its surroundings and hide the snake from its enemies. We call this *camouflage*.

▼This young British adder has colours and patterns which match its surroundings

▲Grass snake pretending to be dead

▲The scarlet king snake of North America is a small constrictor. It has the same bright colours as the poisonous coral snake of the same size

Some poisonous snakes have bright colours and markings to warn away their enemies. Other snakes aren't poisonous but wear bright colours to look dangerous.

Have you ever heard a snake hiss? Most snakes do this to frighten their enemies. Rattlesnakes shake the rattle on the end of their tail to make a warning sound. When an enemy comes too close, many snakes will puff themselves up with air. This makes them look bigger and more dangerous.

After these warnings, a snake will probably bite. Snakes which don't have a poisonous bite sometimes pretend to be dead when they're attacked. They lie on their backs with their mouths open and keep very still.

Hibernation and aestivation

Snakes are cold blooded, so they can't keep warm in cold weather. As a snake gets colder, its movements get slower and slower until it can hardly move at all.

Frost or snow will kill a snake which is out in the open. This is why snakes need to *hibernate* during cold winter weather. They hide underground and rest until spring. Sometimes they use an empty rabbit burrow or hollows around tree roots. The frost can't reach them there.

Before they hibernate, snakes eat as much as they can. The food is stored as fat in their bodies. Snakes don't need to eat during hibernation because they don't use much energy.

▼ Snakes often gather together for hibernation, like these adders

▲Blood python during aestivation

When the cold weather is over, the snakes come out of their hiding places. Spring is their mating season. But they don't eat until they have finished mating. They live on the fat stored up during autumn.

In countries which are warm all year round, snakes don't need to hibernate. They can mate at any time of year. But they do need to rest before mating. This rest is called *aestivation*. It can last from a few weeks to a few months. During aestivation, the snakes keep very still so they don't need to eat.

How young snakes are born

When it is time to mate, the female snake gives off a strong scent. This helps the males to find her. A male and female curl up together in a sunny place and the male smells the female with his tongue. Then the two snakes are ready to mate.

Sometimes, two male snakes will find the same female. They wrestle or bite each other to decide which of them will mate with her.

▼Adders mating

Most young snakes are born (hatch) from eggs. The mother snake lays her eggs a few months after mating. She lays the eggs in rotting wood or a pile of decaying plants. You might find snake eggs in a garden compost heap. Usually, snakes leave their eggs to hatch by themselves. But some coil round their eggs to guard them.

Snakes' eggs don't have hard shells like bird eggs. They are covered with thick skin. The young snake cuts its way through the egg skin with a special tooth on the end of its nose. This tooth drops off when the snake has left the egg.

▲North American gopher snake laying her eggs

North American gopher snake hatching from its egg▶

◀New born Brazilian rainbow boa in its transparent bag

Some snakes don't lay eggs. The mother snake keeps the eggs inside her body until her young are fully formed. The young snakes are born one at a time. Each one is wrapped in a transparent skin like a plastic bag. It breaks out of the bag by pushing with its nose.

Young snakes don't need their mother to look after them. They each go their separate ways. Soon they are hunting and capturing their own food.

◀Brazilian rainbow boa with her young which have just been born

Index

La Loupe

Hodder & Stoughton

A MEMBER OF THE HODDER HEADLINE GROUP

Acknowledgements
Photos: pp. 3, 19 © Neale Haynes/Action-Plus; p. 7 © Steve Bardens/Action-Plus
p. 4 © S. Carmona/CORBIS; p. 16 © Sandy Felsenthal/CORBIS
p. 11 © Popperfoto/Reuters
p. 12 © Holly Stein/Allsport
p. 15 © The Ronald Grant Archive
Cover: © Action Images

Orders: please contact Bookprint Ltd, 130 Milton Park, Abingdon, Oxon OX14 4SB. Telephone: (44) 01235 827720, Fax: (44) 01235 400454. Lines are open from 9.00–6.00, Monday to Saturday, with a 24 hour message answering service. Email address: orders@bookpoint.co.uk

British Library Cataloguing in Publication Data
A catalogue record for this title is available from The British Library

ISBN 0 340 77498 3

First published 2000
Impression number 10 9 8 7 6 5 4 3 2
Year 2005 2004 2003 2002 2001

Typeset by Fakenham Photosetting Ltd, Fakenham, Norfolk.
Printed in Great Britain for Hodder & Stoughton Educational, a division of Hodder Headline Plc, 338 Euston Road, London NW1 3BH by Hobbs the Printers, Totton, Hampshire.

Table des matières

What do you know about basketball?

- Why is it such a fast game to watch?
- How many players are there in a team?
- Can you name any basketball stars?

read on . . .

1. Le jeu

Marc est français.
Il parle du basketball
avec son ami américain, Ed.

Marc Dans mon école,
on joue au football,
mais on ne joue pas
au basketball.

Ed Oh, le basket, c'est super!
C'est un jeu d'action,
un jeu très rapide.

Marc Très rapide?

Ed Oui. On joue contre
l'autre équipe . . .
. . . et contre la montre aussi.

rapide – fast *l'autre équipe – the other team*
contre la montre – against the clock

Ed Ecoute, dans le basketball,
il faut marquer des points.
Il faut envoyer le ballon
dans le panier de l'autre équipe.

Mais quand tu as le ballon,
tu as 24 secondes
pour shooter.
Si tu ne shootes pas,
le ballon passe à l'autre équipe.

Quand une équipe
marque un panier,
l'autre équipe a 5 secondes
pour recommencer.

Marc Je comprends maintenant
pourquoi c'est rapide!

Ed Oui, et l'atmosphère
est électrique.
C'est super, le basket!

il faut – you have to *marquer – to score* *le ballon – ball*
le panier – basket

On marque un panier

L'équipe américaine est championne olympique en 1992

2. Les joueurs

Marc Il y a combien de personnes dans une équipe?

Ed Il y a 10 personnes:
5 joueurs et 5 remplaçants.
Dans un match,
ils changent régulièrement de place.

Marc Qui peut marquer un panier?
Tous les joueurs?

Ed Oui, tous les joueurs peuvent marquer un panier.
Il y a deux avants, un centre, et deux arrières.

Marc Est-ce que les joueurs ont des positions fixes?

Ed Non. Ils changent de position.

un remplaçant – a substitute *tous – all* *un avant – a forward*
un arrière – a guard (plays at the back)

Ed Les meilleurs joueurs
défendent bien,
passent bien,
et ils shootent bien.

Marc Et ils sont très grands . . .

Ed Oui, la taille moyenne
des basketteurs professionnels
est de plus de 2 mètres.*

Marc Incroyable!

Ed Le joueur le plus grand
est Abdul-Jabber,
le basketteur américain légendaire.
Il fait 2,67 m.*
Mais un joueur, Bogues,
fait 1,60 m.*

bien – well *la taille moyenne – the average height* **2 mètres = 6′7″*
le plus grand – the tallest **2,67 m = 7′2″* **1,60 m = 5′3″*

Un match de basketball

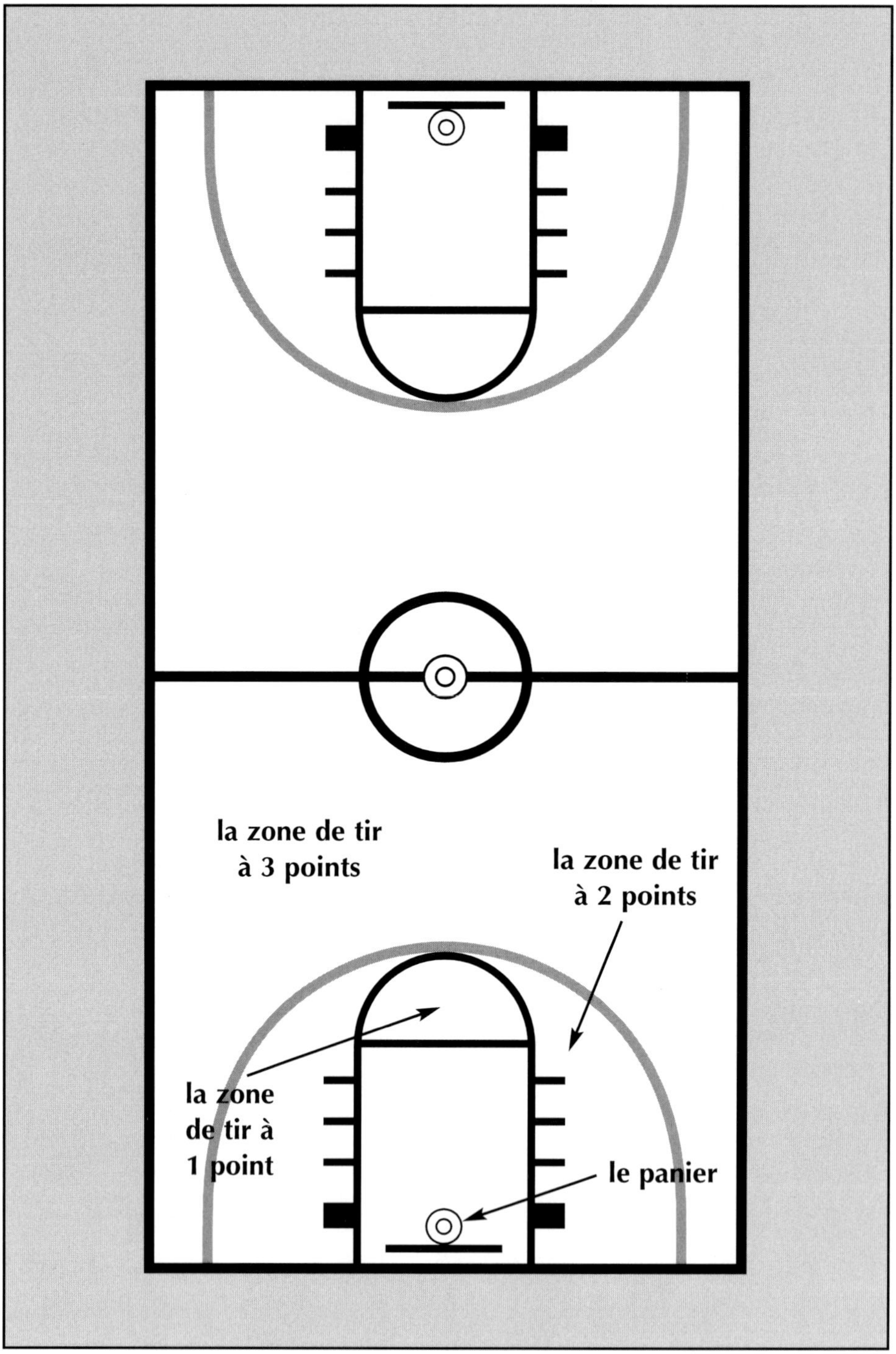

Un terrain de basketball

3. Les points et les fautes

Marc Dis, Ed, c'est combien de points pour un panier?

Ed Un, deux ou trois points – ça dépend de la position du joueur.

Le terrain a trois zones:
- 3 points
- 2 points
- 1 point.

Si le joueur
est dans la zone de tir à 3 points
quand il shoote,
il marque 3 points.

S'il shoote
de la zone de tir à 2 points,
c'est 2 points, etc.
C'est logique!

si (s') – if

Marc C'est grand, le terrain?

Ed Non, le terrain est petit:
28,70 m de long
et 15,20 m de large.
C'est plus petit
qu'un terrain de football.
Donc les fans regardent le match
de très près.

Marc C'est différent du football.
Dans un match de foot,
les spectateurs sont loin
des joueurs.

Ed, le basketball,
c'est un jeu d'action –
est-ce que c'est un peu violent?

Ed Non, non.
C'est un sport sans contact.
Les joueurs ne doivent pas
toucher les autres joueurs.

le terrain – court *près – near* *sans contact – non-contact*
ne doivent pas – mustn't

Les fans regardent de très près

Le basketball est un sport sans contact

Marc Mais ça, c'est impossible!

Ed Impossible, non; difficile, oui!
Mais si on touche un joueur
par accident,
ce n'est pas une faute.

Marc Et si un joueur fait une faute?

Ed Le ballon passe à l'autre équipe.
Après six fautes personnelles
(six fautes de contact),
un joueur est disqualifié.

Marc C'est vrai qu'un joueur
ne doit pas courir avec le ballon?

Ed Oui, tu dois dribbler le ballon.
Si tu arrêtes de dribbler,
tu dois passer le ballon.

une faute – a foul *courir – to run* *tu dois – you have to*
si tu arrêtes – if you stop

4. Les stars du basket

Marc Quel est le meilleur score
d'un basketteur?

Ed Will Chamberlain a le record –
100 points dans un match en 1962.

Et son score moyen
pour la saison,
c'était 50 points par match.
Ça, c'est un record aussi.

Marc Et qui est la plus grande star
du basket?

Ed Ça, c'est Michael Jordan.
Jordan était joueur professionel
de 1984 à 1998.
C'était un vrai champion,
une légende!

meilleur – best *était – was*

Michael Jordan, dans le film *Space Jam*

L'emblème des Chicago Bulls

Marc Quelles sont les meilleures
équipes aux Etats-Unis?

Ed Aux Etats-Unis,
il y a beaucoup de bonnes équipes.
Il y a les Chicago Bulls,
les Houston Rockets et
les Los Angeles Lakers,
par exemple.

Marc Tu vas souvent à des matchs, Ed?

Ed Oui, je vais souvent aux matchs
à l'université.
Tu sais, Marc, la majorité
des joueurs professionnels
commencent à l'université.

Marc A l'université?

Ed Oui. Et beaucoup de joueurs
ne finissent pas
leurs études à l'université –
ils préfèrent jouer au basket.

meilleures – best *commencent – start*

Marc Et ils préfèrent gagner de l'argent,
je suppose!

Ed Oui, c'est vrai.
Un bon joueur, comme
Michael Jordan, par exemple,
peut avoir un contrat
pour 30 millions de dollars!

Marc Les meilleurs joueurs
sont des stars, alors.

Ed Oui. Ce sont de grandes stars.
Le basketteur Shaquille O'Neal,
par exemple,
a fait des albums de rap,
il est dans des films,
et il est dans un jeu vidéo!

gagner de l'argent – to earn money

Il n'est pas nécessaire de jouer dans un club

5. Un sport populaire

Ed On joue au basketball
aux Etats-Unis,
en Europe et en Asie.
C'est plus populaire depuis les
Jeux olympiques de 1992.

Marc Ah oui,
la "Dream Team" américaine
est la championne olympique.

Ed Maintenant, en Angleterre,
il y a des équipes comme
les London Tigers
et les Sheffield Sharks.
Et en France, vous avez
Villeurbanne, Pau-Orthez, etc.

Mais il n'est pas nécessaire
de jouer dans un club . . .

. . . il faut seulement
un ballon et un panier!

depuis – since *il faut – you need* *seulement – only*